Little Hands, Big Dreams

Poetic Reflections on Child Labour

by O.K. Fatai

Published by OK Publishing

Wellington, New Zealand

Email: OK.Publishingnz@gmail.com

Full catalogue in print data may be obtained from the National Library of New Zealand

Dedication

To all those who are facing and fighting the injustices children are going through

CONTENTS

Acknowledgements

I appreciate the help of my family and friends who value the importance of children all over the world and protecting their human rights and overcoming the injustices children are going through.

Lost Dreams

In shadows deep, where innocence does fade,
In fields of toil, where dreams are unmade,
Children small, with eyes so wide,
In the darkness, their dreams they hide.

Tiny hands, so worn and frail,
Bear the weight of an endless trail,
Their laughter silenced, their voices hushed,
In the cruel world, where dreams are crushed.

They should run and laugh and play,
But instead, they toil each day,
Their childhood robbed, their hopes destroyed,
In the darkness, they're left devoid.

Let us rise, take a stand, be bold,
Break the chains that bind, untold,
For every child deserves a chance,
To dream, to hope, to sing, to dance.

In unity, we'll make it right,
Banish child labor from our sight,
For in their dreams, we'll find the way,
To bring forth a brighter, fairer day.

The Hands That Should Create

In the early morning's gentle light,
When the world awakens, pure and bright,
There's a story hidden from our view,
Of the hands that should create, but instead, they toil.

In factories dark and fields so vast,
Children labor, their innocence lost,
Their tiny fingers, nimble and small,
Should paint and draw, but they toil and fall.

They weave the fabric of our days,
Yet their dreams are veiled by endless haze,
Their laughter silenced, their spirits confined,
In the web of labor, their dreams are entwined.

Let us raise our voices, let us unite,
To end this injustice, to make it right,
For every child deserves a chance to thrive,
To sculpt their own dreams and truly come alive.

In the world we envision, together we'll strive,
To ensure that all children survive,
Free from the chains of labor's cruel snare,
With the chance to create, to love, and to care.

Stolen Childhood

In the dim-lit factories, they toil away,
Children robbed of their innocence, day by day,
Their laughter silenced, their dreams denied,
In a world of labor, their childhoods hide.

Tiny hands that should hold pencils with grace,
Instead, grasp tools in a never-ending race,
To weave the garments, craft the wares,
While their youth slips through the world's callous
snares.

We must raise our voices, take a stand,
For these young souls, extend a helping hand,
In unity, we'll break this chain,
And give them back their childhood, free from pain.

Let them run, let them play, let them learn,
In safe spaces, their spirits will return,
No child should suffer, no dreams be marred,
Together, let's ensure their future, unscarred.

The Price of a Penny

In the early morning's muted glow,
Children march to fields where dreams don't grow,
Their hands that should grasp books with delight,
Labor instead, from morning till night.

Beneath the sun's unforgiving glare,
They bear the weight of a life unfair,
Their small shoulders carry heavy loads,
While their dreams remain on distant roads.

Innocence sold for a meager wage,
Their youth spent in a relentless cage,
But we can change this tragic plight,
Together, we can bring back their light.

Let's stand against this dark despair,
With compassion and love, let's declare,
No child should pay the price of a penny,
In their hands, let dreams bloom aplenty.

Chains of the Young

In shadows deep, where hope is rare,
Children toil in silent despair,
Their laughter stifled, their voices suppressed,
In the cruel grip of labor's conquest.

Tiny hands that should paint the skies,
Weave instead a web of lies,
In factories dim and fields so vast,
They carry burdens meant to last.

Innocence lost to the grinding wheel,
As dreams are crushed 'neath the world's ordeal,
But we shall rise, we shall defend,
The rights of children, we'll amend.

Let's break the chains that hold them tight,
Illuminate their world with hope's pure light,
For every child deserves to be free,
To chase their dreams and just be.

The Lost Childhood

In the quiet dawn of a world so cold,
Where dreams should bloom and tales be told,
There exists a darkness we must bear,
Children's labor, their burdens to share.

Their little hands, once meant to play,
Now toil through night and day,
In the relentless grip of endless toil,
Their childhood dreams begin to spoil.

We must stand tall, we must unite,
To end this blight, to set things right,
For every child deserves to thrive,
To laugh, to learn, to truly come alive.

In their eyes, we'll find the way,
To break the chains and bring the day,
When child labor is but a tragic tale,
And every child's dreams will set sail.

The Silent Tears

In a world where innocence should reign,
A haunting truth inflicts a lasting pain,
Children toil in shadows, faces worn,
Their dreams and laughter slowly torn.

Tiny hands that long for toys and games,
Bear the weight of life's relentless claims,
In fields, in factories, they stand so small,
With innocence lost, they bear it all.

But we, as one, can make a stand,
To free them from this harsh demand,
Together we can break the chain,
And give these children life again.

Let their laughter fill the air,
With dreams and hope beyond compare,
For in their joy, we shall find the way,
To bring forth a brighter, fairer day.

The Lost Playground

Beneath the sun's unforgiving glare,
Children toil, burdened beyond compare,
Their tiny hands, meant for games and art,
Instead, play a role that breaks the heart.

Innocence stolen by labor's cruel hand,
Dreams buried deep in the shifting sand,
But we, as a world, can take a stand,
To free them from this harsh, relentless land.

Let's unite to break their chains,
End the suffering, ease their pains,
For every child, a chance to thrive,
To chase their dreams, to feel alive.

In a world where childhood's pure and bright,
Let's ensure their futures are set alight,
With love and hope, we'll clear the way,
To bring them back to the lost playground, they'll play.

The Lost Innocence

In the realm of shadows, young souls confined,
Children toil in silence, dreams undermined,
Their laughter silenced, their spirits chained,
In the world of labor, their youth detained.

Tiny hands that should hold books with delight,
Grasp instead tools in the fading light,
Their dreams, like stars, so distant and high,
In the depths of labor, they wither and die.

But we, united, can break the chains,
End the suffering, dissolve the pains,
For every child, let's forge a new way,
To restore their innocence, come what may.

In the heart of darkness, let's bring the dawn,
Let childhood dreams and hopes be reborn,
With love and care, we'll take a stand,
To free each child from labor's cruel hand.

The Price of Tomorrow

Beneath the weight of a world that's cold,
Children bear burdens far too bold,
Their tender shoulders, frail and small,
Should carry dreams, not labor's thrall.

In factories dim and fields so wide,
They labor ceaselessly, side by side,
Their faces marked with weary lines,
Innocence lost to the grinding grind.

Together, let's raise our voices high,
In unity, let's reach for the sky,
For every child, a chance to reclaim,
The lost joys of childhood, their rightful aim.

In a world where love and compassion prevail,
No child should wear the laborer's frail,
With open hearts, let's make a decree,
To end child labor, set the young ones free.

Chains of Childhood

In the realm of innocence, where dreams should thrive,
Children labor, just to stay alive,
Their laughter muffled, their eyes grow dim,
In the cruel grip of labor's grim.

Tiny hands that should sculpt with clay,
Stack bricks, stitch fabrics, each day,
Their hopes held captive, their spirits confined,
In the world of toil, their dreams maligned.

But we, as one, can break the chain,
End their suffering, release their pain,
For every child, let's take a stand,
To free them from labor's cruel hand.

In unity, we'll find the way,
To bring forth a brighter, fairer day,
Where childhood's joys, so pure and sweet,
Shall once again dance to the youthful beat.

The Lost Playground

In the playground of youth, where laughter should ring,
Children, in labor's grasp, their voices do not sing,
Their playgrounds stolen, dreams out of sight,
In the world of toil, they lose their light.

Tiny hearts that should chase butterflies,
Count pennies, not stars in the skies,
Their innocence tarnished, their childhoods confined,
In labor's shadow, their dreams are maligned.

But we, as a world, can take a stand,
Extend a loving, helping hand,
To break the chains, to set them free,
And let them reclaim their lost glee.

In the lost playground, we'll find the way,
To bring back the joys of a brighter day,
Where every child can laugh, learn, and play,
In a world where their dreams have the final say.

Shadows of Innocence

In the quiet corners of a weary world,
Where innocence in shadows is unfurled,
Children toil with heavy hearts and hands,
Bound by labor's cruel and unforgiving demands.

Tiny souls that should dream and soar,
Are trapped in a cycle of endless chore,
Their laughter stifled, their spirits worn,
In the dark realm of toil, they're torn.

But together, let's break this chain,
End the suffering, the endless strain,
For every child deserves a chance to bloom,
To escape the shadows and dispel the gloom.

In unity, we'll seek the light,
To restore their dreams, their stolen right,
For in their hope, we shall find the way,
To bring forth a brighter, fairer day.

The Price of a Penny

Beneath the weight of a world so stern,
Children's hearts and dreams often burn,
Their tiny hands, meant for games and play,
Bear the burdens of another day.

In factories dim and fields so vast,
They labor on, from first to last,
Innocence lost to the grind of toil,
As dreams become entangled in the soil.

But we can stand, together strong,
To right this tragic, unjust wrong,
For every child deserves a chance to soar,
To dream, to learn, to explore.

In their bright eyes, we'll find the way,
To break the chains and bring the day,
When child labor is but a distant sorrow,
And their dreams can flourish, bright tomorrow.

The Silent Struggle

In the hidden corners of a world so vast,
Children toil in shadows, a burden unsurpassed,
Their laughter silenced, their hopes denied,
In the cruel embrace of labor, they reside.

Tiny hands, once meant to sculpt and play,
Now bear the weight of a relentless day,
Their dreams, like stars, so distant and faint,
In the world of toil, they slowly wane.

But together, let's break this chain,
End their suffering, their silent pain,
For every child deserves a chance to bloom,
To escape the darkness, dispel the gloom.

In unity, we'll light the way,
To restore their dreams, come what may,
For in their innocence, we shall find,
The strength to leave child labor behind.

The Lost Voices

In a world where childhood should brightly gleam,
Children's voices are lost, it would seem,
In factories and fields where shadows creep,
They labor tirelessly, their innocence they keep.

Tiny hearts that should dance and sing,
Carry burdens instead, a heavy thing,
Their dreams, like kites, should take to the sky,
But in labor's grasp, they wither and die.

But we can stand, together as one,
To undo the harm that's been done,
For every child deserves a chance to play,
To dream, to hope, to learn their way.

In their eyes, we'll find the key,
To unlock a world where they're truly free,
Where child labor is but a painful memory,
And their voices can ring out in joyful harmony.

Dreams in Chains

In the quiet corners of a weary world,
Where innocence is slowly unfurled,
Children toil in silence, hearts so sore,
Their dreams entangled in labor's lore.

Tiny hands, meant for games and mirth,
Grasp tools and burdens from birth,
Their laughter muffled, their spirits confined,
In the world of toil, their dreams maligned.

But together, we can break this chain,
End their suffering, dissolve the pain,
For every child deserves a chance to dream,
To escape the darkness, let their hopes gleam.

In unity, we'll find the way,
To bring forth a brighter, fairer day,
Where childhood's joys, pure and sweet,
Shall once again dance to life's youthful beat.

The Lost Playground

In the playground of youth, where laughter should
prevail,
Children's voices silenced, their hopes frail,
Their innocence stolen, their dreams denied,
In the world of labor, they quietly subside.

Tiny hearts that should skip and sing,
Instead bear burdens, to labor they cling,
But we, as a world, can take a stand,
Extend our love, lend a helping hand.

Let's break the chains, set them free,
Reclaim their laughter, let their spirits be,
In the lost playground, we'll find the way,
To bring back the joys of a brighter day.

For every child deserves to laugh, to play,
To chase their dreams, to feel the sun's warm ray,
In a world where their voices can ring out,
And the lost playground of youth, without a doubt.

Innocence in Chains

In the shadows of a world unkind,
Innocence lost, young souls confined,
Children toil with weary hearts and eyes,
Their dreams entangled in labor's cruel guise.

Tiny hands that should craft dreams anew,
Bear the burdens that adults should pursue,
Their laughter muted, their spirits oppressed,
In the world of labor, they're seldom blessed.

But together, we can break their chains,
End the suffering, ease their pains,
For every child deserves a chance to rise,
To reclaim their dreams beneath the open skies.

In unity, we'll light the way,
Bring back the joy of a brighter day,
For in their hope, we'll find the key,
To a world where every child can be free.

The Lost Childhood

In a world where youth should brightly gleam,
Children's hopes are shattered, it would seem,
In factories and fields where shadows creep,
They labor on, their innocence they keep.

Tiny hearts that should dance and play,
Carry burdens through night and day,
Their dreams, like stars, should light the way,
But in labor's grasp, they slowly decay.

But we, as one, can stand and fight,
To end the wrong, to make things right,
For every child deserves to soar,
To dream, to learn, to explore.

In their eyes, we'll find the way,
To break the chains and bring the day,
When child labor is but a distant sorrow,
And every child's dreams can shine tomorrow.

The Price of a Penny

Beneath the weight of the world's demands,
Innocent children in toil's harsh hands,
Tiny souls, once free to dream and roam,
Now trapped in labor's unforgiving home.

Their tender hands, meant for games and play,
Now grasp tools through night and day,
Their dreams, like birds, should take to flight,
Yet in the cruel world, they're kept from sight.

But together, we can break their chains,
End the suffering, dissolve their pains,
For every child deserves to bloom,
To escape the darkness, to dispel the gloom.

In unity, we'll find the way,
To restore their dreams, come what may,
For in their innocence, we shall find,
The strength to leave child labor behind.

Shadows in the Factory

In factories' shadows, where dreams should thrive,
Children toil, just to stay alive,
Their laughter silenced, their hopes denied,
In the world of labor, their dreams are cast aside.

Tiny hands, once meant to hold a kite,
Now bear the weight of a never-ending fight,
Their childhood stolen, their spirits bound,
In the realm of toil, their joy can't be found.

But we, united, can break this chain,
End their suffering, release the pain,
For every child deserves a chance to gleam,
To escape the shadows, to chase their dream.

In their eyes, we'll find the way,
To bring forth a brighter, fairer day,
Where childhood's joys, so pure and sweet,
Shall once again dance to life's youthful beat.

The Lost Innocence

In the world where dreams should brightly bloom,
Children toil in shadows, in a silent gloom,
Their laughter hushed, their spirits dimmed,
In the harsh grip of labor, their innocence trimmed.

Tiny hands, meant for games and mirth,
Bear burdens heavy since their birth,
Their dreams, like flowers, struggle to grow,
In the realm of toil, where shadows flow.

But together, we can break their chains,
End their suffering, release their pains,
For every child deserves a chance to rise,
To reclaim their dreams, reach for the skies.

In unity, we'll find the way,
To bring back the light of a brighter day,
For in their hope, their resilience so wild,
We'll discover the strength to reunite the child.

The Playground of Youth

In the playground of youth, where joy should reside,
Children's laughter silenced, dreams pushed aside,
Their innocence stolen, their freedom encaged,
In the world of labor, their lives are staged.

Tiny hearts that should skip and sing,
Now bear burdens of an adult-like thing,
But we, as one, can take a stand,
To offer love and lend a helping hand.

Let's break their chains, set them free,
Rekindle their laughter, let their spirits be,
In the lost playground, we'll find the way,
To bring back the joys of a brighter day.

For every child deserves to laugh, to play,
To chase their dreams in the sun's warm ray,
In a world where their voices can be heard,
And the lost playground of youth, fully restored.

The Burdened Heart

In the realm of innocence, where dreams should sprout,
Children bear burdens, without a doubt,
Their laughter muffled, their hopes concealed,
In labor's harsh grip, their dreams are repealed.

Tiny hands, meant for games and play,
Grasp tools and chores, no time for a day,
Their youth is stolen, their spirits confined,
In the world of toil, their dreams maligned.

But we, together, can break the chain,
End their suffering, alleviate the pain,
For every child deserves a chance to bloom,
To escape the darkness, let their dreams consume.

In unity, we'll find the way,
To bring forth a brighter, kinder day,
Where childhood's joys, so pure and mild,
Shall once again thrive, in the heart of the child.

The Playground of Lost Dreams

In the playground of youth, where joy should ring,
Children's voices silenced, no songs to sing,
Their innocence stolen, their hopes in decline,
In the world of labor, they slowly resign.

Tiny hearts, once filled with dreams so vast,
Now carry burdens, from first to last,
But we, as a world, can take a stand,
Extend our love, lend a helping hand.

Let's break their chains, set them free,
Restore their laughter, let their spirits spree,
In the lost playground, we'll find the way,
To bring back the joys of a brighter day.

For every child deserves to laugh, to play,
To chase their dreams in the sun's warm ray,
In a world where their voices can be heard,
And the lost playground of youth, fully restored.

The Chains of Poverty

In the shadowed corners of despair,
Childhood's innocence, so rare,
Bound by poverty's relentless hold,
Children bear burdens, young and bold.

Tiny hearts, once full of glee,
Now face a life of misery,
Their dreams, like stars, remain afar,
In the grip of poverty's chilling spar.

With empty stomachs and tattered clothes,
They face a world that seldom shows,
Compassion and care for those in need,
As they labor on, their young hearts bleed.

But let us rise, with hearts aflame,
To break the cycle, change the game,
For every child, let's clear the way,
To a brighter future, where they'll have their day.

A Child's Labouring Tears

In the world where poverty's grip is tight,
Children labor from morning till night,
Their innocence lost in the struggle to survive,
In the depths of despair, they strive.

Tiny hands, meant for play and mirth,
Toil on, right from their birth,
Their dreams, like fragile glass, they hold,
But poverty's chains are strong and bold.

In a cycle of need, they're caught,
With little to eat, and dreams untaught,
But together, we can break the chain,
End the suffering, alleviate the pain.

Let's bridge the gap, lend a hand,
Help them escape poverty's cruel strand,
For every child deserves a chance to thrive,
To chase their dreams, to truly come alive.

The Weight of Poverty

In the shadows cast by fortune's glare,
Children toil in a world unfair,
Their small shoulders bear a heavy load,
As poverty's grip takes hold.

Tiny hands, meant for games and dreams,
Grasp tools instead, by harsh regimes,
Their laughter silenced, their spirits confined,
In the bleak world of labor, they're resigned.

Innocence lost to the relentless fight,
As they toil from morning until night,
But we, united, can break their plight,
Bring hope to their dark and endless night.

Let's rise as one, lend a helping hand,
To uplift these children from poverty's land,
For every child deserves a chance to soar,
To dream, to learn, to explore.

The Silent Tears of Childhood

In the realm of poverty's cruel reign,
Children's tears fall like gentle rain,
Their laughter buried beneath despair,
As they labor on, their dreams threadbare.

Tiny hearts, once filled with delight,
Face a world devoid of light,
Their dreams, like petals, withered and torn,
In poverty's grasp, they're sadly worn.

But we, as a world, can make a stand,
Extend our love, lend a helping hand,
To break the chains that bind them tight,
And lead them to a future that's bright.

Let's erase their tears, dispel their sorrow,
Secure their dreams for a hopeful tomorrow,
For every child deserves a chance to thrive,
To escape poverty's grip and truly come alive.

Other books by O.K. Fatai

1. Poems on Values to Succeed Worldwide in Life: Being Responsible
2. Poems on Values to Succeed Worldwide in Life: Courage
3. Poems on Values to Succeed Worldwide in Life: Good Families
4. Poems on Values to Succeed Worldwide in Life: Forgiveness
5. Poems on Values to Succeed Worldwide in Life: Good Friends
6. Poems on Values to Succeed Worldwide in Life: Grace
7. Poems on Values to Succeed Worldwide in Life: Hope
8. Poems on Values to Succeed Worldwide in Life: Humility
9. Poems on Values to Succeed Worldwide in Life: Joy
10. Poems on Values to Succeed Worldwide in Life: Justice
11. Poems on Values to Succeed Worldwide in Life: Life
12. Poems on Values to Succeed Worldwide in Life: Love
13. Poems on Values to Succeed Worldwide in Life: Mercy
14. Poems on Values to Succeed Worldwide in Life: Peace
15. Poems on Values to Succeed Worldwide in Life: Perseverance
16. Poems on Values to Succeed Worldwide in Life: Faith
17. Poems on Values to Succeed Worldwide in Life: Harmony with Nature
18. Poems on Values to Succeed Worldwide in Life: Education

More books by O.K. Fatai

1. Poems on Values to Succeed Worldwide in Life: Understanding and Wisdom
2. Poems on Values to Succeed Worldwide in Life: Work and Optimism
3. Poems on Values to Succeed Worldwide in Life: Adversity and Confidence
4. Poems on Values to Succeed Worldwide in Life: Listening and Diversity and Unity
5. Poems on Values to Succeed Worldwide in Life: Sharing and Honesty
6. Poems on Values to Succeed Worldwide in Life: Simplicity and Harmony
7. Poems on Values to Succeed Worldwide in Life: Unity in Diversity and Connections
8. Poems on Values to Succeed Worldwide in Life: Contentment and Acceptance
9. Poems on Values to Succeed Worldwide in Life: Excellence and Compassion
10. Poems on Values to Succeed Worldwide in Life: Generosity and Being Passionate
11. Poems on Values to Succeed Worldwide in Life: Gentleness and Trustworthy
12. Poems on Values to Succeed Worldwide in Life: Patience and Being Tactful
13. Poems on Values to Succeed Worldwide in Life: Purity and Integrity
14. Poems on Values to Succeed Worldwide in Life: Being Modest and Persistence
15. Poems on Values to Succeed Worldwide in Life: Respect and Loyalty

About the Author

O.K. Fatai is a poet and author from Wellington, New Zealand. He likes to spend time writing poems, especially ones that explore the different aspects of values and virtues that are widely accepted in different cultures today.

O.K. Fatai enjoys writing songs and some of his forthcoming books are song lyrics that look at different values and virtues and some of their appeal to us today. In his spare time, he writes short stories and novels. He is looking forward to sharing these stories with readers around the world, and he has already published some short stories and has more than ten forthcoming publications in children's literature. O.K. Fatai is writing novels for young adults and adults. He is also a playwright and has written, produced and directed more than fifteen short plays.

He likes painting abstract art and enjoys the different interpretations of abstract paintings, especially when they reflect values and virtues. He is a photographer who likes to take photographs of nature and the environment, which has a special place in his heart. He is keen on filming and editing videos, plays musical instruments and is part of a local band.

O.K. Fatai is a volunteer at the United Nations and regional prisons in Wellington and, for many years has volunteered to more than ten other organizations. He works in the health sector and is a consultant for three different online companies, and the President and CEO of more than three businesses. He is also available as an external consultant to the United Nations, the European Bank for Reconstruction and Development, and the Asian Development Bank.